My Body is MY Body

By Allison Schmitt
Illustrated by Neris Naranjo

WestBow Press books may be ordered through booksellers or by contacting:

WestBow Press
A Division of Thomas Nelson & Zondervan
1663 Liberty Drive
Bloomington, IN 47403
www.westbowpress.com
844-714-3454

Interior Image Credit: Neris Naranjo

ISBN: 978-1-6642-2604-3 (sc)
ISBN: 978-1-6642-2606-7 (hc)
ISBN: 978-1-6642-2605-0 (e)

Library of Congress Control Number: 2021904470

Print information available on the last page.

WestBow Press rev. date: 4/28/2021

WESTBOW
PRESS®
A DIVISION OF THOMAS NELSON
& ZONDERVAN

This book and this body
belong to _____

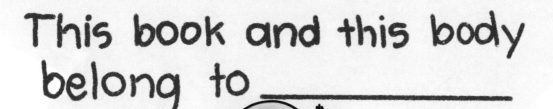

To my sister,
the most courageous
woman I know
-A.S.

Dedicated to Emma,
Mariví, Lucca
and José Eduardo.
Be Brave.
-N.N.

My body is MY body. It belongs to me.

Nobody can touch it, except for me.

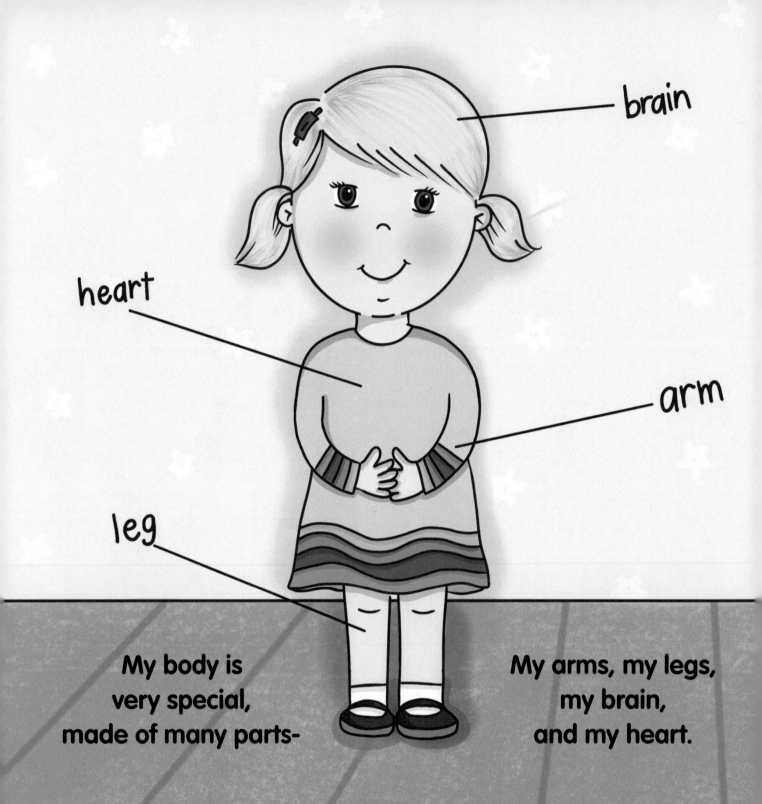

brain

heart

arm

leg

My body is
very special,
made of many parts-

My arms, my legs,
my brain,
and my heart.

Some parts are visible and you can see,
But some are hidden and are just for me.

You can see my feet, my head, my face,
But you cannot see my private place.

These places are very special
and have different names.
Girls have breasts and a vagina,
but boys are not the same.

CHANGING
ROOM

They have a penis
down below,
And these are areas
others may not go.

We all have a bottom
in the back,
Another place others
cannot look at.
We cover these areas
with our clothes.
If someone tries to see
them, we tell them NO.

If they say you have to
and you don't know
what to do,

You tell them NO,
your body's just
for you.

If it's your dad, your uncle, a pastor, a preacher,
A friend, a babysitter, coach or your teacher,

A stranger, a relative, it doesn't matter who,
Your body is YOUR body and it belongs to you.

Find someone safe and
tell them right away.
They'll take care of you and
listen to what you have to say.

Your body is YOUR body.
It belongs to you.
Nobody can touch it,
except for you.

Sometimes your mommy
helps to wash
and keep you clean,
But she must
keep you safe in those
places unseen.

Sometimes a doctor has to check to see
If your body is well and
all is healthy.

But in the room
your mommy must stay.
To make sure the doctor
treats you the right way.

Our bodies are special
and one of a kind.

They're made up of many parts
and a beautiful mind.

My body is MY body.

It belongs to me.

Nobody can touch it,

except for me.

Your body is YOUR body.
It belongs to you.

Nobody can touch it,
except for you.

Information
for
Parents

TALK TO KIDS
ABOUT BODY SAFETY & BOUNDARIES

As a caregiver, you can and should talk openly about our bodies and healthy boundaries with your kids. This helps build a strong bond that will make you the "go-to-person" when they have questions or if a situation arises.

So, how do you get this conversation started? If you're feeling unsure, take a deep breath. We promise you feel more uncomfortable than they do! The most important thing is to make sure your kids understand that no matter what happens, they can share with you without fear of being blamed and that you will protect them.

Below are a few ideas to get started:

- ❑ Tell them they can tell you anything & you will believe them.

- ❑ Use proper names for private parts.

- ❑ "Sometimes touch might just feel uncomfortable, even if you like the person. If it's uncomfortable, you can say no."

- ❑ "You don't have to hug or kiss anyone if you don't want. Not even grandma. How about a high five instead?

- ❑ "It's not okay for someone to ask you to touch their private parts with any part of your body, including your mouth."

- ❑ "No one should ever touch you where a bathing suit covers." This is a good visual, especially for young children.

- ❑ "Your whole body is a private part whenever you want it to be. You get to decide who touches you."

- ❑ "No one should ask you to keep a secret. If they do, you should tell me."

 **DARKNESS TO LIGHT**®
END CHILD SEXUAL ABUSE

Learn More at www.D2L.org

5 STEPS TO PROTECTING OUR CHILDREN™

One in 10 children in the U.S. will be sexually abused before the age of 18. As adults, we are responsible for the protection of the children in our care.

The 5 Steps to Protecting Our Children™ is an introductory guide to help adults protect children from sexual abuse. Using an evidence-informed approach, these steps provide simple and practical actions you can take to prevent, recognize, and react responsibly to child sexual abuse. Together, they form the framework for Darkness to Light's prevention training program, *Stewards of Children*®.

THE 5 STEPS TO PROTECTING OUR CHILDREN™

STEP 1: LEARN THE FACTS

1 in 10 children are sexually abused abused before their 18th birthday. This means realities rather than blind trust should influence our choices regarding children's safety from sexual abuse. 90% of children who are sexually abused know their abuser. Sexually abused children are at greater risk for psychological, emotional, social and physical problems, often lasting into adulthood.

STEP 2: MINIMIZE OPPORTUNITY

More than 80% of child sexual abuse incidents occur when children are in isolated, one-on-one situations with adults or other youth. Choose group situations and have multiple adults supervise children. Make sure interactions can be observed and interrupted. Ask for protective best practices in schools and organizations that serve your children, including background checks, personal and professional reference checks, and a code of conduct for staff and volunteers.

STEP 3: TALK ABOUT IT

Open conversations with children about body safety, sex, and boundaries is one of the best defenses against child sexual abuse. Talk with children when they are young, and use proper names for body parts. Tell children what sexual abuse is, and when age appropriate, about sex. Tell children what parts of the body others should not touch. Use examples with situations and people in their lives. Teach children that they have the right to tell any person "NO" to unwanted or uncomfortable touch.

STEP 4: RECOGNIZE THE SIGNS

Know the signs of abuse to protect children from further harm. Physical signs are not common, but the following should be carefully examined by a professional: bruising, bleeding, redness, rashes, bumps or scabs especially around the genitals; urinary tract infections; chronic stomach pain, headaches or other ailments that can't be explained medically. The most common symptoms of child sexual abuse are emotional or behavioral changes, including withdrawal, depression, and anger. Signs don't always mean sexual abuse, but signs can be a reason to take more interest in the child.

STEP 5: REACT RESPONSIBLY

Understand how to respond to risky behaviors and suspicions or reports of abuse. There are three reasons we need to react to sexual abuse: **disclosure, discovery, and suspicion**. Few reported incidents are false.

Disclosure: A child has broken through secrecy, fear, and shame and has chosen you as the person he or she trusts enough to tell. Honor that with attention, compassion and belief. Listen calmly and openly. Tell the child you believe him/her. Don't ask leading questions about details. Seek the help of a professional who is trained to talk with the child about sexual abuse.

Discovery: You've witnessed a sexually abusive act by an adult or youth with a child, or you know by some other way that abuse has taken place. For example, a friend or coworker may have told you something definitive. In cases of disclosure or discovery, report immediately to local law enforcement or to child protective services in the county in which the child lives.

Suspicion: You've seen signs in a child, or you've witnessed boundary violations by an adult or youth toward a child. Suspicion means, at a minimum, you need to set some limits or ask some questions.

HOW CAN I LEARN MORE ABOUT PROTECTING CHILDREN?

Prevention training for adults creates a culture of awareness. It gives people the skills to create safer environments. It makes them more willing to intervene in unsafe behaviors by adults with children.

Stewards of Children® is a program that teaches adults to:

- Prevent sexual abuse before it can happen.
- Recognize signs of sexual abuse in children.
- Recognize unsafe behaviors by adults.
- React responsibly when a child discloses, or when an adult discovers or suspects sexual abuse.

Visit www.D2L.org to learn more about *Stewards of Children®*, see where it is being offered in your area, or find ways to get your community involved in a grassroots initiative to end child sexual abuse.

DARKNESS TO LIGHT

1064 Gardner Road, Ste. 210 | Charleston, SC 29407 | 1-843-965-5444 | www.D2L.org

This information is intended only as a supplement to Darkness to Light's Stewards of Children® training, which provides in-depth learning, tools, and practical guidelines to help adults prevent, recognize, and react responsibly to child sexual abuse. For more information on Stewards of Children®, visit www.D2L.org/Stewards.

Printed in the United States
by Baker & Taylor Publisher Services